A Newbie's Guide to OS X Maver

Switching Seamlessly from Windows to M

Minute Help Guides

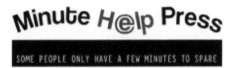

SOME PEOPLE ONLY HAVE A FEW MINUTES TO SPARE

Minute Help Press

www.minutehelp.com

© 2013. All Rights Reserved.

Cover Image © EpicStockMedia - Fotolia.com

Table of Contents

Introduction: It Just Works

So you've decided to take the plunge and get started with OS X Mavericks for Mac. Congratulations! Longtime Mac users know that Mac just works – the interface you'll come to know and love is intuitive, powerful, and designed to make your life easier. Technology can and should be exciting, and your Mac will offer all of that excitement, without the headaches!

Whether you're a first time Mac user or a seasoned Mac devotee, OS X Mavericks has something for everyone. For starters, Mavericks introduces Books and Maps for the desktop – two favorites of iOS users. The Safari web browser and Mac Finder are more intuitive than ever – Finder introduces tabbed browsing and tags, making it easier than ever to find, organize and manage your files and folders. You can now store all your Mac-created passwords in iCloud so that you can access them on other devices. And with over 200 new features to explore, you'll be glad to know that Mavericks will help your machine be as fast, efficient, and battery-conservative as possible. With OS X Mavericks, Apple also took a revolutionary approach to OS upgrades by offering it absolutely free of charge, so there's truly no good reason not to upgrade.

But wait, you say. You've never used a Mac before, and you're already lost. No worries! This guide was written just for you. We'll cover everything you need to know about making the switch from Windows to Mac, the basic terminology you'll need to find your way around and customize your machine, some handy tips and tricks that even serious Mac users may not know, and some basic maintenance that will keep your Mac happy and healthy for years to come. Finally, we'll cover a number of free third party apps that will help you get the most out of your Mac and OS X Mavericks. Along the way, we'll give you lots of screenshots, tips and practice so that you can feel confident, competent and comfortable with your new Mac.

Congratulations on choosing OS X Mavericks for Mac – now let's get started!

How to Use This Guide

This guide will introduce you to your Mac and to many of OS X Mavericks' new features. If you're brand new to OS X, you may want to read through **Part 1: Making the Switch** in order to get your bearings. Then, try working through **Part 2: The Basics.** Try to keep your Mac on as you read so that you can try out features and tasks as you read about them. The key is to engage your muscle and visual memory as you read. This will help you remember things a little more clearly and help you connect your Mac's features to the things you need or want to do with your machine. Don't be afraid to experiment, either! The more you explore your Mac, the more comfortable you'll feel.

After you've made it through Parts 1 and 2, look over **Part 4: Maintaining Your Mac**, to get a sense of how to keep your Mac healthy and happy.

Part 3: Getting the Most Out of Mac and **Part 5: The Power of Free** may serve you better as reference sections rather than chapters you read straight through from start to finish. There's a lot of information here, and be careful not to overload yourself. These sections have plenty of information for seasoned Mac users as well.

If you do start feeling overwhelmed, take a break! Rome wasn't built in a day, and you shouldn't push yourself to learn everything Mac in one day either. We promise, though, it'll come fairly quickly. Have fun with the process – Mac is easy to use, and we know you'll enjoy it!

Part I: Making the Switch from Windows to Mac

You are no doubt aware of the passionate nature of the Mac versus Windows[1] debate. However, the two operating systems are much less at odds with each other than their respective devotees can seem to be, so don't worry! While it's true that OS X Mavericks looks quite a bit different from Windows, rest assured that you'll be able to accomplish just about everything you could do in Windows on your Mac and more.

This section will outline the major differences between the Windows and OS X operating systems, give you a crash course in "Mac speak," help you find your way around a Mac keyboard, and give you some tips for migrating your files from a Windows system to a Mac running OS X Mavericks.

NOTE: This guide is based on OS X Mavericks, the newest version of OS X. However, some of this information applies to older versions of the software like Lion and Mountain Lion. If you're running Lion or Mountain Lion though, we strongly recommend installing Mavericks, available free in the App Store.

1.1 Introducing Mac OS X

Windows and Mac OS X are two types of operating systems. Operating systems are major pieces of software that control just about every aspect of a computer user's experience. OS X Mavericks is the latest version of Mac OS X. The operating system OS X has been around since 2001, and we've already seen Cheetah, Puma, Jaguar, Panther, Tiger, Leopard, Snow Leopard, Lion and Mountain Lion. With each upgrade, Mac has become more powerful, user-friendly, and easier for former Windows users to come to terms with. In OS X 10.9, Apple is breaking with its big cat naming tradition to offer a powerful new operating system that should do its notorious surf break namesake proud.

While Mavericks is packed with exciting new features like iBooks and Maps, some of the most impressive aspects of the update aren't quite as visual. Mavericks will help you get the most out of your Mac by improving speed and battery life. It introduces App Nap, which will slow down an apps' power consumption when they're open but not in use. Memory compression will also help you make the most of your storage space by compressing files and folders you don't use often. There are a number of boosts built right in that will preserve your battery and improve performance, without requiring a bit of your valuable attention. Of course, there's much more to Mavericks, and we'll tell you all about it in the pages to come!

Vertical Integration

For the average end user, the main difference between Mac and Windows is the user interface – what you see and how you interact with your machine. We'll be covering this in detail throughout this guide. However, another important difference between the two is more fundamental. Mac OS X is designed to run on Apple computers – and only Apple computers, legally speaking. Windows,

---

[1] Windows computers are often referred to as PCs. PC actually stands for "personal computer." The term originally had nothing to do with Windows or Microsoft!

meanwhile, can be run on several different brands of computers – Dell, Toshiba, HP, etc. You can even run Windows on a Mac if you just can't bear to give it up!

However, Mac users benefit immensely from Apple's vertical integration. Your Mac's hardware and software are optimized for each other, resulting in better performance and less startup "junk" that frequently comes preinstalled on machines running Windows. Mac's famous intuitiveness also has roots in its seamless software and hardware design.

Apple's long history of vertical integration also put it in an enviable position when mobile computing took the world by storm. In fact, OS X Mavericks introduces even deeper integration throughout the Apple iDevice family (iPhone, iPad, iPod, etc.). If you use other Apple devices, OS X Mavericks can help you seriously streamline your content and workflow across all of your Apple devices.[2]

A Note About Compatibility

Programs, or, in Mac-speak, applications (apps for short) are smaller pieces of software that rely on your operating system to run correctly. This means that a Windows version of Microsoft Office won't work on a Mac computer – instead, you'll need Microsoft Office for Mac. Don't panic, though, if you're not ready to spend your hard-earned money repurchasing major software like MS Office – we'll discuss some free alternatives in **Part 5: The Power of Free**.

Long story short, when you install new programs, you'll be looking for Mac-compatible ones. In the past, this could be quite limiting, but due to Mac's surge in popularity, most programs are now available in Mac versions.

File Formats

Your Mac is going to handle most of your Windows files without any drama. There are, of course, exceptions. WMV (Windows Media Video) and WMA (Windows Media Audio) files will play on your Mac, but you may need to do some tinkering if you want to manage them using iTunes.

For the most part, though, Mavericks will make file migration a breeze. The Migration Assistant Tool can be run during setup or later on, and we'll show you how in **Part 2.1**.

Now that you've got a basic understanding of the big-picture differences between OS X Mavericks and Windows, let's get a little more specific, starting with some terminology.

1.2 A Computer Task By Any Other Name…

Mac and Windows look quite different, but underneath the new look and feel, you'll find that the tasks you need to perform are fairly similar. You will need to master some new vocabulary, though.

The following table is a rundown of some frequently used Mac/Windows terms. Feel free to refer back to this table as often as you need to!

---

[2] Apple mobile devices run an operating system called iOS. OS X Mavericks plays very nicely with iOS, but they're not quite the same thing.

Windows	Mac
Windows Explorer / My Computer	Finder
Control Panel	System Preferences
Programs	Applications (often shortened to apps)
Task Bar / Start Menu	Dock
Tray	Menulets
Recycle Bin	Trash
My Documents / My Photos / etc.	Documents / Photos / etc.

1.3 Keyboard, Trackpad and Magic Mouse

Ok, enough theory! Now let's get into some mechanical differences that will affect the way you interact with your computer.

Keyboard

Apple Key

Obviously, there's no Windows key on a Mac keyboard – instead, you've got an Apple key (⌘), which doubles as the command key. You'll find it just to the left of your spacebar. For keyboard shortcuts, it works just like the CONTROL key on a Windows keyboard - ⌘+c (copy), ⌘+v, (paste), for example. You may hear it referred to as the "pretzel key" or the "clover key", though older Mac keyboards used an actual Apple image instead of the twisty symbol.

Control Key

The Mac control key is there for right click functionality. Ignore what you may have heard – you can and should "right click" on a Mac. One way to do this is to hold down the CONTROL key and click. Try it and see how it works!

Delete (Backspace)

On a Windows keyboard, the backspace is a 'backwards delete' (removing the space immediately preceding the cursor) and the 'delete' is a 'forwards delete' (removing the space immediately after the cursor). On a Mac keyboard, the backspace key is labeled 'Delete' and is in exactly the same location as the Windows backspace key. The Windows delete key (forward delete) is labeled 'Del ->.' On smaller Mac keyboards, this key does not exist. You can still forward delete by using the FN+Delete if you must.

Function Buttons

On a Mac, it's easy to tell what each function button does by the tiny picture assigned to the button. On newer Mac keyboards, F1 dims, F2 brightens, F3 opens Mission Control, F4 opens Launchpad, F5 dims backlit keyboards, F6 brightens backlit keyboards, F7 skips back a track, F8 pauses/plays media, F9 skips forward a track, F10 mutes, F11 decreases volume, and F12 increases volume. Go ahead and play with these function buttons. You won't hurt anything, we promise!

Magic Mouse / Trackpad

Traditional PC-based mice allow users to move the cursor/pointer around the screen, click, drag and drop, and maybe scroll. However, in OS X Mavericks, the mouse and trackpad have some major additional capabilities that you'll want to get the hang of pretty quickly.

If you're using a magic mouse, you'll find one seamless top surface in place of the standard right and left buttons. While you will still use the mouse to move the cursor and pointer around within documents and apps, you can also use the entire surface of the mouse as if it were a trackpad. This allows Mac users to take advantage of multitouch gestures (see **2.3** for more).

And by the way, if you're feeling a little overwhelmed with all of this information, don't panic – it will all become second nature to you with a little practice. With that in mind, let's get started using your Mac!

Part 2: The Basics

Ready to get started using your Mac? This section will give you what you need to get up and running. So go ahead and fire it up by pressing the power button!

2.1 Setup Assistant

The first time you start a new Mac, you'll need to do some setup. OS X Mavericks makes this incredibly easy, but here's what you'll need to know.

1. First, you'll need to **select your country** (if you don't see yours, choose "See All").

2. Next, you'll choose your **keyboard layout** – if you're an English speaker in the United States, you'll probably be most comfortable with the U.S. keyboard, but if you're, say, working on a doctorate in Chinese literature, there are options for you, too.

3. After you click continue, you can **choose a wireless network**.

4. If you do select a wireless network, it will trigger **Migration Assistant**. Migration Assistant will help you transfer files from an older Mac, a backup disk, or a Windows PC. Migration Assistant will automatically move files into their appropriate locations – music files to the Music folder, for example.

5. Next, you can allow or disallow **location services**. Location services allow applications to "see" where your computer is physically and provide you with relevant content (map and recommendation services come to mind).

6. The next screen prompts you to enter an **Apple ID**. If you don't already have an Apple ID, you can create one from this screen. It's a good idea to go ahead and set this up – it's free and will allow you to take advantage of the App Store and iTunes. Plus, it will allow you to set up iCloud - a must for Apple mobile device users!

7. Almost there! Read **the terms of service** and click **Agree**.

8. Next, if you've entered an Apple ID, you can **set up iCloud**. iCloud is "the cloud done right," according to Apple's website. Installing iCloud on your Mac means that your pictures, music, applications, email, calendars, contacts, and more are stored "in the cloud." Apple will automatically sync them with all of your iCloud-running Apple devices. No more sync headaches! What this means is that if you add a name to your contacts on your Mac, that name will automatically be pushed to your iPhone Contacts. Similarly, if you purchase a song on iTunes on your iPod, it will automatically be delivered to your Mac. And in Mavericks, iBooks is along for the iCloud ride as well. We strongly recommend that you go ahead and

enable iCloud, whether or not you own other Apple devices at the moment (be warned: they tend to multiply).

9. The next part of the setup process is **Find My Mac**, powered by iCloud. Find My Mac is exactly what it sounds like. If your Mac goes missing, Find My Mac will allow you to pinpoint its physical location, send messages to it, wipe its contents, and lock it. Hopefully you will never need this feature, but if you do, you'll be glad you enabled it.

10. And finally, here we are at your **account creation** screen! Enter your full name, account name, and password. The first account you create on your Mac is an administrative account by default. Be sure to pick an account name you can live with, because this will be very difficult to change in the future.

11. Now **select your time zone**.

12. Decide whether or not to send Diagnostics and Usage Data to Apple.

13. Decide whether or not to register your installation of Mavericks with Apple.

14. **Start Using Your Mac** – this is where the fun really starts!

2.2 Meet Your Mac

So here you are, staring at the vast expanse of your empty desktop. If you're a former Windows user, you may feel a little disoriented by all that wide-open screen space. So let's take a tour – it's nowhere near as barren as it appears!

You should be seeing something like this (without the three red labels of course):

Menu Bar

At the top left, you'll see the menu bar. This is the only menu bar on your Mac, and the contents of the bar will change based on what application you are running. Right now, it's displaying the Finder menu (remember that Finder is the Mac equivalent of Windows Explorer).

Menulets

At the top right, you'll see several "menulets" – backup status, Bluetooth, wireless connectivity, volume, battery, time and date, the name of the account currently logged in, Spotlight, and Notifications. Go ahead and click through the menulets – you won't hurt or change anything, and it's good to know what each one does. Pay special attention to the magnifying glass (Spotlight) and Notification Center (the last menulet on the right). You'll probably be using these two often, once you're off the ground with your new Mac.

Dock

At the bottom of the screen, you'll see the Dock, a strip of icons that provide quick access to frequently used applications. It's easy to customize, so once you've got a sense of the apps you use the most often, you'll be able to design a tailor-made dock just for you.

Use your trackpad or magic mouse to hover over each of the pictures in the Dock to see which applications the pictures represent. You'll see, from left to right, Finder, Launchpad, Mission Control (if you've updated from a Mac running Mountain Lion), Safari, Mail, Contacts, Calendar, Reminders, Notes, Maps, Messages, FaceTime, Photo Booth, iPhoto, iTunes, iBooks, App Store and System Preferences. We'll talk about them all soon!

To start an app from the dock, simply click on the icon. If an app is currently running, a tiny spotlight will appear underneath the corresponding icon. If you click on an icon while the application is open, doing so will bring the application window to the front of your screen. You may notice a light gray line on your dock. This is the "dividing line." To the left of this line are apps and to the right are folders, files, documents and the Trash bin. OS X Mavericks' Dock also includes a download manager. Clicking on this will cause a list of recently downloaded files to pop up.

Trash

At the right end of all the applications on your Dock is the Trash. To delete a folder, file or application, drag the item to the Trash, or right click the item and select 'Move to trash' from the pop-up menu. If you want to eject a disk or drive (such as an iPod or USB flash drive), drag the volume into the Trash. As the volume hovers over the trash, the icon morphs from a trash can to a large eject button. Release the mouse, and your volume has been ejected. To empty the trash, right click on the Trash Can in the Dock, and select **Empty Trash.**

2.3 Swipe-aerobics: Multitouch Gestures on the Trackpad/Magic Mouse

Before we go any further, you're going to need to know how to interact with OS X Mavericks. So, limber up your wrists, because we're going to do some multitouch gesture swipe-aerobics!

Chances are you already know one "gesture" – clicking. Your Mac will happily respond to single and double clicking, just like your PC. Now, let's add something new to your repertoire – the tap.

Tap

Tap once somewhere on your desktop, using either the surface of your magic mouse or your trackpad, depending on your Mac. This is a tap, and it's the same as a click.

Double Tap

Now, tap with two fingers at the same time. Did a menu just pop up? That's because you just "right clicked" on your desktop! Remember, you can also "right click" using CONTROL+click – feel free to use whichever option works best for you.

Scroll

To scroll, move up and down in documents or side to side with two fingers (two-finger swipe). Doing so also activates the scroll bar which otherwise remains hidden in apps like Safari and Finder. Scrolling all the way to the top or bottom creates a 'rubber band' effect, where the page bounces down or up depending on whether you have reached the top or bottom of the page. You may already be familiar with this effect from iDevices and apps, such as Safari on the iPhone or iPad.

TIP: OS X Mavericks defaults to "natural scrolling," in which content follows the direction of your fingers. This has received mixed reviews. If you decide to turn it off, check out Trackpad Options in 3.3.

Swipe

Swiping should be very familiar for anyone who's used an e-reader or an iPad or iPhone. In OS X Mavericks, we need to practice two types of swipes.

First, take three fingers, put them on your trackpad or magic mouse surface, and drag them to your right. This should appear to move your whole desktop out of the way and drag in your Dashboard area (we'll explore widgets and the Dashboard in **3.2**). Later, you'll be using the three-finger swipe across to navigate between full screen apps as well.

Now, take three fingers and swipe **up.** This triggers Mission Control. It lets you see everything that you have running. Right now, that's not much, but once you've got six or seven applications going, it can be a productivity lifesaver! Take three fingers and swipe back down to return to your desktop.

In short, "swiping" just means dragging your fingers either across or up and down the track pad. In OS X Mavericks, you'll want to be comfortable with three- and two-finger swipes. You'll use two-finger swiping in Launchpad and Safari, in addition to using it for scrolling (**2.6**).

Pinch

In some applications, you can "pinch" to zoom in and out. Take your thumb and forefinger and move them toward each other in a pinching motion. This will zoom in on pictures and web pages. The reverse motion will zoom out. You can also pinch to reveal all of your Safari tabs (**2.6**).

Five Finger Pinch

Pull all five fingers together to reveal Launchpad – a list of all the apps on your Mac that looks suspiciously like iOS. Move all five fingers apart from each other to dismiss it. We'll talk more about Launchpad in **2.6.**

Rotate

Rotate images using your thumb and first finger and twisting your wrist in the direction you'd like to rotate.

2.4 Tutorial: Getting to Know Your Mac with Photo Booth

Alright, now we're ready to delve a little deeper into your Mac! We're going to use Photo Booth as an example to learn how to run applications in OS X Mavericks.

Find the Photo Booth icon on your Dock (shown above). Click it to open the application. Notice how it starts bouncing? That means that the program is opening. Once it stops bouncing, you'll see a small white light under the icon, indicating that the app is running.

Running an Application

Now you should be staring at yourself! Surprise! Photo Booth uses your Mac's built-in webcam to take still pictures or video. It also includes a range of goofy effects (click on Effects to see them). Go ahead and have a little fun with the camera button – don't worry if the pictures are embarrassing. We'll talk about deleting files in a little bit.

TIP: See the green light in the top center of your monitor? That lets you know that your webcam is running.

Let's talk about how to manage this application. In OS X Mavericks, you'll use two areas of the screen to handle your application. First, and most obvious, is the application window itself. In Photo Booth, this is the window where you found the effects and hopefully took a picture or two. Second, you'll use the application's menu bar.

Inside the application window, in the top left corner, you'll see a little red button and a little yellow button. The red button will close the window (like the red X in Windows), and the yellow button will minimize it. Click the yellow **Minimize** button. Notice how Photo Booth shrinks down to your Dock? Every time you minimize something in Mavericks, it's sent to your Dock. Maximize Photo Booth again by clicking the active Photo Booth icon on the right side of your Dock.

Now, look at the top left menu bar. See where it says "Photo Booth" in bold? You'll also see **File, Edit, View, Camera, Window, and Help.** These menus change depending on what application you're using. You can also minimize the window from here. Click **Window,** and then **Minimize.**

NOTE: From here on out, when we talk about consecutive clicks through menu items, we'll write them like this: **Window > Minimize.**

Do you see how the window itself is minimized, but the Photo Booth menu bar is still displayed at the top of the screen? Use the menu bar to quit the program by clicking **Photo Booth > Quit Photo Booth.** You'll need to get into this habit. In most Mavericks applications, you can close an application window without exiting the application itself. Imagine that you're working on three Microsoft Word documents. If you close all three documents, you're still running the application Microsoft Word, and you'll need to use **Word > Quit Word** to fully exit.

Now, reopen Photo Booth by clicking on the icon in the Dock. Go ahead and delete any pictures you don't want to keep by clicking on the thumbnails in the bottom part of the screen, and then using the little black x that appears in the corner.

TIP: you'll see that little black x throughout Mavericks. It always means "delete."

Running Full Screen Applications

Now, in the menu bar, click **View,** and then **Enter Full Screen.** You can also use the two gray arrows in the top right corner. Your app is now running in Full Screen Mode! Take a few minutes to practice the three-finger swipe between the full screen Photo Booth window and your desktop.

To exit Full Screen, simply press the **ESC** key in the top left of your keyboard, or move your mouse to the top of the screen to recall the menu bar. Use either the blue square in the right corner or **View > Exit Full Screen** to exit. The screenshot below is a full screenshot!

Sharing from Applications

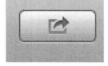

One more thing to notice in Photo Booth: see that little box with an arrow coming out of it right above the thumbnails? You'll see it in your applications and even in your Finder window. You can share through email, Twitter, Flickr and more, depending on the accounts you've set up, which we'll get into later (**3.1**). It's a handy connectivity feature in the age of social networking!

Before you close Photo Booth, look through the menu bar to see what else you can do! Feel free to open some of the other applications on your Dock as well – don't worry if you don't understand everything yet. Don't forget to practice closing each application using the menu bar.

2.5 Getting Around Using Finder

Now that you've got a general idea about how to run applications, let's talk about file management. Chances are, you have lots of pictures, documents, movies and other files that you'd like to store on your Mac. If you used Migration Assistant during setup, those files may even be in place already. In order to find them, you'll use Finder, the Mac equivalent of My Computer or Windows Explorer.

Finder is the default menu bar you'll see at the top of your screen. You can also open Finder from the Dock. Look for the smiling puzzle piece and click on it.

This will open a **Finder window**. You can open as many Finder windows as you like (this is useful if you need to copy or move files from one folder to another).

Let's take a look at the anatomy of a Finder Window. You should be seeing something like this on your screen right
now:

Take a minute to locate the various components of your own Finder window.

Views in Finder

There are four ways to view folders on your Mac, including icons, lists, columns and Cover Flow. Different views make sense for different file types, and you can change the view using the View options icons (pictured on the left).

Cover Flow View

In this example, the view is set to "Cover Flow," as indicated by the icon at the top (similar to "Film Strip" in Windows). This is great for looking through pictures or music albums when you need a slightly larger size than icon view gives you. You can also sort by clicking on the column headers.

Icon View

Icon view can help if you need to sort through several image files or applications. It gives you either a thumbnail of a picture or an application icon.

List View

List view, on the other hand, gives you more information about the file, including the date it was last modified. This is a great view for sorting. While you can sort in any view using the sort options button, in list view you can also sort files by clicking the column headers ("Name," "Date Modified," etc.).

Column View

Finally, column view is great when you need to see a file's path. It shows the folder hierarchy a file is located in. Notice that Finder doesn't include the Windows "go up one level" button – Column View is a good way to get the same results and navigate easily through your file structure.

Sorting in Finder

Finder gives you a number of ways to sort your files and folders. You can sort by name, type, application required for opening the file (like Microsoft Word, for example), the date the file was opened, modified, or created, the file size, and, in Mavericks, tags. This is a handy feature if you're looking for something specific – that giant image file your sister sent you last month, or the spreadsheet you were working on a few minutes ago. You can also sort by clicking column headers if you're in List view.

File Management

Most file management tasks in OS X are similar to Windows. Files can be dragged and dropped, copied, pasted and cut. If you need to create a new folder, use the gear icon in Finder, which will give you the option you need.

Favorites

If you look on the left side of the Finder Window, you'll see a Favorites sidebar. This section includes high-frequency folders, like Documents, Pictures, Downloads, and more. It also includes "All My Files," which is exactly what it sounds like!

You'll also see your Applications folder in your Favorites panel. Go ahead and open it up. Every application on your computer doesn't have to take up valuable screen real estate on your Dock. If you install an application and don't add it to your Dock, your applications folder is one way to find it and open it. (though we do think Launchpad is a faster method – more on this soon!).

To add an application or file to your Favorites menu, just drag it over to the Favorites menu and drop it. To remove an item from Favorites, right-click it and select **Remove From Sidebar.**

Spotlight

Spotlight is OS X Mavericks' search tool, and it's always at your fingertips. It's the little magnifying glass next to your account name in the top right, and the white search box in the top right of your Finder window. Click on it to search for files on your computer. In Mavericks, you can also search for tags here.

Practice: Open a new Finder window by clicking the Finder icon on the dock. Experiment with the back and forward buttons, the four view options, the Finder tasks, and the sort options. See what you can find in your Applications folder. If you used Migration Assistant, see what it moved to your Music, Pictures, and Documents folders. Try to find the Share button. Click it to see your sharing options, whether or not you'd like to share anything right now.

Tabbed Browsing

Mavericks introduces tabbed browsing in Finder windows – it's a handy feature that can keep your workspace a little less cluttered. To open a second Finder tab, press COMMAND+t, or click **File > New Tab**. This will allow you to have multiple Finder windows open inside one frame. This can be quite useful if you need to look at a couple of different Finder screens, but you may still prefer multiple Finder windows for dragging and dropping tasks.

Of course, even with this feature, you may accidentally find yourself drowning in open Finder windows. If this happens, it's easy to consolidate everything. Just click **Window > Merge All Windows** in the Finder menu bar to bring everything together.

Tags

A very exciting new feature in Mavericks OS X is the ability to tag your files and folders inside Finder. You'll find your tags in the left menu in Finder. There are several color tags, as well as Home, Important, and Work. To assign a tag, simply right click a file or folder and then click the tag you'd like to use. If you'd like to assign a new tag, right click the item, click tags, and then type the name of your new tag in the white box. After you create a new tag, you can use it again and again, and it will appear on the list of tags (you may need to click **Show All** to reveal it). This is a great way to keep yourself organized, especially with projects that may have files scattered throughout your content libraries.

2.6 Other Need-to-Know Applications in Mavericks

Now that you've got the hang of running applications and managing files and folders in OS X Mavericks, let's cover some other basics.

Launchpad

Launchpad is the rocket ship icon right next to the Finder puzzle piece on your Dock. Go ahead and click it. You're now looking at a list of all the applications stored on your computer. It's a lot easier to get to Launchpad than it is to navigate to the applications folder in Finder. The Launchpad aesthetic will probably also remind iPad, iPhone and iPod users of their mobile devices (and this isn't coincidental). Every application you download is automatically added to Launchpad.

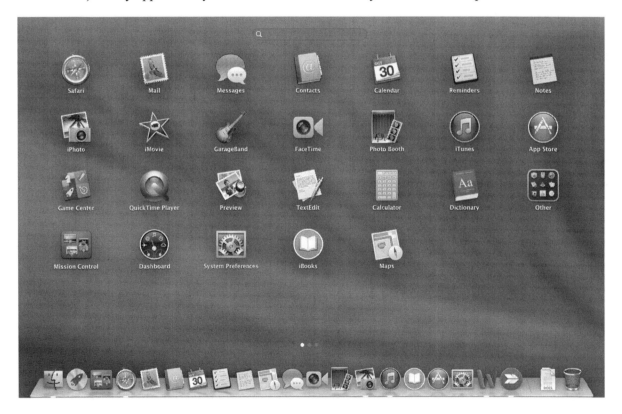

You can arrange your Launchpad however you'd like by clicking and holding icons and moving them around. You can see how many screens there are in your Launchpad by looking at the series of dots at the bottom. There are three screens in the Launchpad shown above – again, this design element is very similar to home screens on iOS.

To move between screens, use two fingers to swipe left and right. For a review of swiping, check **2.3**. Serious app users can use the Spotlight search box at the top of Launchpad to find an app quickly, no matter how many others are installed!

Mission Control

Mission Control is the icon right next to Launchpad on your Dock. You can click the icon on the Dock, or use three fingers to swipe up. Mission Control lets you see everything you have running and makes it easy to switch apps or navigate between full screen apps. In the Mission Control screenshot below, the user is running Photo Booth in full screen mode, with iPhoto, Microsoft Word, a Finder Window and Safari running on the Desktop. Switching to any of these apps is as simple as clicking on it!

Safari

Speaking of Safari, the OS X Mavericks upgrade includes some major tweaks to Apple's proprietary web browser, making it faster and smarter than ever. Safari now features **Shared Links**, an easy way to see sites being shared by people you follow on Twitter. It's also significantly **less power-hungry** – Apple claims that you can surf about an hour longer in Safari than other web browsers. Apple has also beefed up **privacy and security controls,** so that you can control how much of your online activity is public. Safari supports the Do Not Track standard and includes a feature called Private Browsing which will not store your web history or allow cookies or saved forms. Safari also includes powerful features for web developers in Web Inspector. Features introduced in 2012's Mountain Lion OS include a dual-purpose address/Google search bar, similar to Google Chrome, a built-in **Share button**, and an **offline reading list**. Tabbed browsing now includes multitouch gesture support, so that you can **swipe between tabs**. **Pinch to reveal your tabs** in tab view, and use two fingers to swipe between tabs while you're there. The screenshot below shows a user swiping between tabs in tab view.

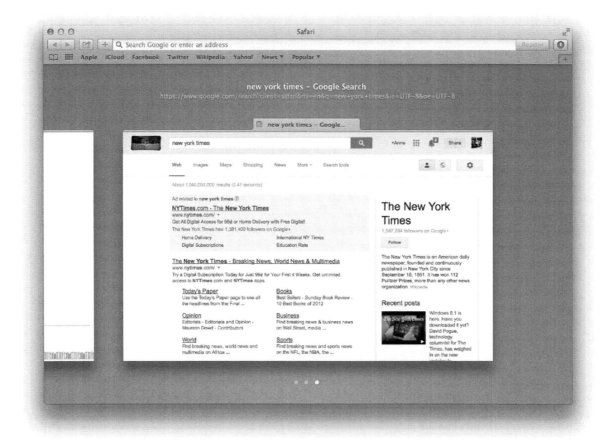

When you're not in tab view, you can use a two-finger swipe in place of the browser's back and forward buttons. Try it out and see what you think!

If you've enabled iCloud, you can also **use iCloud tabs** in Safari. This allows you to send your open tabs to iCloud, so that you can open Safari on a different Apple device and pick up right where you left off.

OS X Mountain Lion introduced major improvements in Safari's **password management system**. The browser will now ask if you'd like passwords saved and filled in for you the next time you visit (incidentally, never a good idea on a shared computer!), and also includes a password panel, where you can actually view all of your saved passwords, instead of maddening little black dots, by entering your system password. In the Safari menu bar, choose **Safari > Preferences,** and then click **Passwords** to keep up with your saved passwords.

In Mavericks, however, Safari goes a step further with **iCloud Keychain.** Saved passwords are great, but passwords that are synced across multiple devices are even better. Best of all are unique, impossible to guess passwords saved and synced!

To use iCloud Keychain, be sure it's enabled under **System Preferences > iCloud**. You'll have to set up a security code that you'll use to enable the feature on other Apple devices. Once this feature is enabled, Safari will suggest passwords for you. Of course, the caveat here is that some sites request that passwords not be saved or won't allow Keychain to generate a password. The other possible issue is that you need to be able to remember passwords on other computers that may not run Safari. Nevertheless, it's a useful feature that may save you hours of time that would otherwise be spent on Forgot Your Password? links.

The App Store

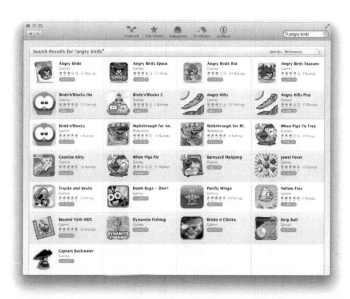

The App Store is the place for purchasing Mac apps (or finding free ones!). We've put together a list of some of our favorite free apps in **Part 5: The Power of Free,** and many of them are available in the App Store.

To be clear, not every Mac-compatible program can be downloaded from the App Store. However, many of them can, and the App Store is ridiculously easy to use!

Open the App Store from the Dock, then search for an app using the search box in the top right of the App Store. When you find an app you'd like to install, click either the word **FREE** or the price next to the app title. Then click **install**. You'll be prompted to enter your Apple ID and password. You must have an Apple ID to use the App Store.

While the app is installing, you can keep an eye on its progress by watching the blue progress bar underneath the Launchpad icon in the Dock. When the blue bar completes and disappears, your new app is ready to use!

This section should have given you enough information to get started with OS X. However, there's much more to discover. Read on to learn more about advanced features in OS X Mavericks!

iTunes

Along with the original iPod, iTunes brought Apple into the media business way back in 2001. Since then, it's grown to encompass audiobooks, podcasts, movies, television shows, and more. In Mavericks, it's as easy to use as ever.

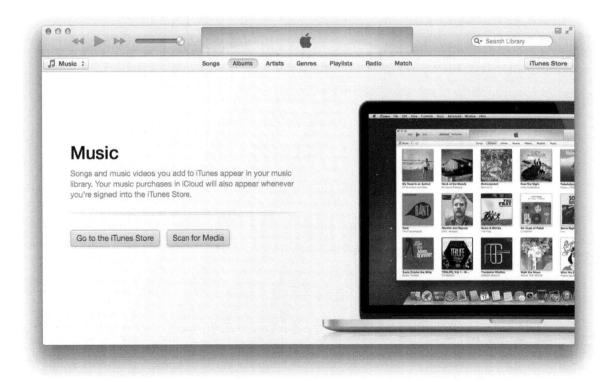

Of course, Apple would prefer that you purchase *all* your music through the iTunes store (accessible from the top left corner of the iTunes media player). Fortunately for those of us with large CD collections, you don't have to. iTunes makes it reasonably easy to import your music. The first time you open the app, you can click **Scan for Media** to locate media files already on your computer.

You can also transfer music from your CD collection to your iTunes library if your Mac has a CD drive. Just insert a music CD and let iTunes do the rest! When asked if you'd like to rip the CD, say yes. iTunes will then analyze the CD and automatically download artist and track information, if you're connected to the internet. If you'd like to manually enter information for songs, right click them and click Get Info.

Once your music and movie libraries are set up, you can enjoy them using iTunes. You can sort your music by song, album, artist, or genre. You can also create your own playlists, or rock out to some of Apple's default offerings, which include things like "90s music" and "top twenty-five most played." You can also create Genius playlists. Genius playlists analyze the song that you've chosen to base your playlist on and gather similar songs from your library. We've always been surprised at what an eerily good DJ iTunes can be!

To create your own playlists, click Playlists at the top of the iTunes window. Then, click the plus sign in the bottom left corner. Give your playlist a name, and then start adding music. Drag and drop the songs you'd like to add into the playlist panel. You can always remove them by right clicking them and clicking "Delete." Bear in mind that deleting an item from a playlist does not delete it from your computer.

In OS X Mavericks, iTunes includes iTunes Radio – a much-loved feature of iOS 7. iTunes Radio should have streaming radio services like Pandora shaking in their boots. iTunes Radio is a worthy competitor. It works similarly to Pandora. To create a new station, just click the plus sign and enter a song, artist, or genre you want to build a station around. iTunes Radio will then play similar music, keeping track of the songs and artists it selects for you. Of course, Apple makes it very quick and easy to purchase those songs from the iTunes Store, should you choose to do so!

If a large portion of your music library comes from sources other than iTunes and if you have other Apple devices, you may be interested in iTunes Match. It costs $24.99 a year, and will store your entire music library in iCloud. This will allow you to stream your music collection from other Apple devices on demand. This is definitely worth it if most of your music predates your new Apple allegiance!

iBooks

iBooks is new to OS X Mavericks, though it's been available for iOS users for some time. It's essentially iTunes for books, and with over two million books to choose from, it's a powerful platform for bookworms.

iBooks works very similarly to iTunes. The app itself displays your personal library with a link to the store in the top corner. In the store, you can choose from bestsellers, free books, and more. You can also use the categories link to find popular titles in your favorite genres.

If you've purchased any iBooks titles on other iOS devices, you'll be able to sync them with your Mac. iBooks may be the most useful for students – it may not be as comfortable to read on a computer screen, but it's certainly much easier to take notes with a full keyboard!

In the screenshot below, you'll see the opening pages of *Alice in Wonderland* by Lewis Carroll. If you look at the top, you'll see basic controls for returning to your library (the book icon), seeing the table of contents, and navigating your notes. In the right corner, you'll be able to adjust the font size, search, and add bookmarks.

CHAPTER I.
DOWN THE RABBIT HOLE

ALICE WAS BEGINNING TO GET VERY TIRED OF SITTING BY her sister on the bank, and of having nothing to do: once or twice she had peeped into the book her sister was reading, but it had no pictures or conversations in it, 'and what is the use of a book,' thought Alice 'without pictures or conversation?'

So she was considering in her own mind (as well as she could, for the hot day made her feel very sleepy and stupid), whether the pleasure of making a daisy-chain would be worth the trouble of getting up and picking the daisies, when suddenly a White Rabbit with pink eyes ran close by her.

There was nothing so VERY remarkable in that; nor did Alice think it so VERY much out of the way to hear the Rabbit say to itself, 'Oh dear! Oh dear! I shall be late!' (when she thought it over afterwards, it occurred to her that she ought to have wondered at this, but at the time it all seemed

To add notes and highlights, simply highlight text by dragging with your mouse. This brings up options to add a note or highlight a passage in the color of your choice. It's a great way to annotate your reading material, and iBooks in iOS will make taking copious notes much easier than a touchscreen can. Of course, your notes, highlights, bookmarks, and last page read will be synced across all of your devices running iBooks.

In the Mavericks version of iBooks, you can also quiz yourself on your reading comprehension using Study Cards. Study Cards are based on items you search for or highlight, and it's a quick and easy way to study. No more index cards!

FaceTime

Think an iPhone is the only Apple device you can use to make calls? Think again! Your Mac includes the FaceTime app, which will turn your Mac into a full-fledged video phone. FaceTime is very similar to Skype, though you'll only be able to call contacts that own Apple devices with FaceTime installed. It's a great way to stay in touch with friends and family who are far away. Just click on the FaceTime camera to get started!

The first time you open FaceTime, you'll be prompted to sign in with your Apple ID. You can associate your FaceTime app with a phone number, an email address, or both – whatever you think will be the easiest for your contacts. After everything's set up, you'll see a list of your Contacts. Contacts with FaceTime capability will show a FaceTime camera icon next to their names.

To call someone on FaceTime, just click his or her name (or use the search bar to find them). Then click the FaceTime button to initiate the call. When you're finished, just click the End button in the window.

iWork and iLife

If you are lucky enough to have a brand new Mac or MacBook, then the iWork and iLife suites ship free with your machine. iWork includes Pages, Keynote and Numbers (word processing, presentations, and spreadsheets, respectively), and iLife includes iPhoto, iMovie and GarageBand. These are all extremely powerful programs each deserving of their own guide. Unfortunately, those of us who downloaded Mavericks on older computers will still have to pay for these in the App Store.

Part 3: Getting the Most Out of Mac

Now that you've got a good grip on how to get around and manage your Mac, let's take a more in-depth look at the features that will help you get the most out of OS X Mavericks. This section will introduce you to the many ways Mavericks will give you more freedom, flexibility, and computing power.

In this section, we'll cover adding mail accounts, some of the other native applications in Mavericks, tips for customizing your machine, tips for security and privacy, and a handy list of keyboard shortcuts. This is the section that will help you make your Mac your own.

3.1 Mail, Contacts and Calendars

OS X Mavericks offers powerful Mail, Contacts and Calendars features to help you get and stay organized. You can synchronize your existing accounts with these native features, and we think you'll enjoy the native app experience much more than web-based mail and calendars!

Adding Accounts

To add accounts, go to **System Preferences** on your Dock (the gears icon) and select **Internet Accounts.** From here, you can add accounts that haven't already been migrated, including iCloud, Exchange, Google, Twitter, Facebook, LinkedIn, Yahoo!, AOL, Vimeo and Flickr. Adding accounts here will start populating Mavericks' native Mail, Contacts, Reminders and Calendar apps and adding options to your Share button.

*Note: You can also add accounts within the Mail, Contacts, Calendars, and Reminders apps by opening each app and clicking **File > Add Account**. We prefer the System Preferences method because it covers several bases at once!*

To add accounts, just click the type of account you'd like to add and enter your login credentials.

Follow the prompts to add accounts to the appropriate OS X Mavericks apps.

Once you've added your accounts, you can start using **Mail, Contacts, Calendar, Messages and Reminders**, all located on your Dock. If you've enabled iCloud, these apps will all stay synced with their counterparts on your Apple mobile devices. These apps also communicate with your Notifications Center (**3.2**), so that you can keep track of all of your incoming notifications in one unobtrusive spot without needing to open several separate applications.

Twitter, Facebook, LinkedIn, Vimeo and Flickr

OS X Mavericks supports deep Twitter, Facebook, LinkedIn, Flickr and Vimeo integration. To get started, simply sign in to your account from **System Preferences > Internet Accounts**. Select Twitter, Facebook, LinkedIn, Flickr, or Vimeo, and then enter your username and password. From now on, you'll be able to use that account with the Share button throughout Mavericks and receive notifications in your Notifications Center.

After adding your social media accounts, you can post to them straight from your desktop using the Notification Center in the very top right corner. In Mavericks, you can send a message, tweet, or post to Facebook or LinkedIn here.

Using Mail

Mail is very easy to use after you've added all your accounts. The Notification Center will help you be sure you never miss another message, and the Mail app will help you organize the daily barrage so that you see the most important messages.

The mail app will pull in existing folders for you. It also gives you the ability to set up VIP senders, like your mother or your boss, so that you don't miss the most important communications.

To write a new email, click the new message icon in the top left (it's the square and pencil icon). This brings up the new message screen, where you can enter recipients' addresses, attach files, and of course, write your message. When everything looks good, just click the paper airplane icon in the top left corner.

Note: The October 2013 version of Mavericks caused some fairly serious headaches for Gmail users who wanted to sync their Google accounts with Apple Mail. At the time of writing, Apple is working on a fix. In the meantime, Gmail users may be happier using webmail!

Using Calendar

Mavericks' Calendar app received a fantastic redesign, and we think it's easier to use than ever. Calendar, like Mail, pulls in your existing calendars from Google, Facebook, and more, so that everything you need to show up for shows up in one location. Calendar will also keep you up to speed with upcoming holidays and Facebook friends' birthdays. Like most other apps in Mavericks, Calendar syncs between Mavericks and all your iOS devices, so you'll always know what's going on.

To add a new event in Calendar, click the plus sign in the top left corner or double click the day you'd like to add the event. From there, you can ad a location for the event, invite your contacts, and add notes, attachments and links.

In Mavericks, Calendar also includes some new and potentially very useful features. Map previews for recognizable locations. It can also calculate how long it will take you to get to a location and send you a notification when it's time to leave. You can also see the weather report for a location at the time an event is scheduled, so you'll know what to wear.

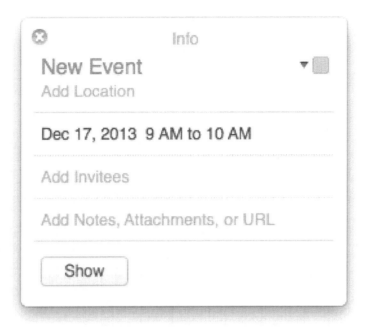

Using Contacts

Contacts are also pulled in from your synced internet accounts. We found our Facebook contacts were a little overwhelming, so we used **System Preferences > Internet Accounts** to remove them. Your mileage may vary, of course.

Contacts is very simple to use. Your contacts appear in an alphabetized list, with as much or as little detail as you'd like to add. Like most other apps, you can add new contacts using the plus button, and anything you add will be synced across your Apple device family. In Mavericks, thanks to the new Maps app, you can also see a map to a contact's address.

There are quite a few more fields here than it seems at first. Each field with arrows can be changed – for example, clicking "home" next to Email reveals home, work and other, as well as custom.

3.2 Other Native Features and Apps in OS X Mavericks

Notification Center

The Notification Center, located at the top right of your screen, unifies your reminders, calendar alerts, email and social networking notifications, Game Center messages and more. This feature was introduced in OS X Mountain Lion, and it's received some significant improvements in Mavericks.

Notification Center gives you a comprehensive view of what's going on in your electronic life. In Mavericks, you can respond to many notifications in the Notifications Center. Notifications are also organized by app. Of course, in today's digital world, it can feel like there's a new notification every second – if you need to focus, you can set Do Not Disturb Mode by pressing Option and the + key simultaneously. This will cause the Notifications icon to display grayed out. The same keystroke will reactivate it.

TIP: *Notification Center makes a noise every time a new notification is received. If it's starting to get to you, you can turn off the sound for each notifying app under **System Preferences > Notifications.** You will need to turn off sound for each individual app.*

Game Center

Mountain Lion finally added Game Center (formerly limited to iPhone, iPad, and iPod Touch) to the OS X experience, and it hasn't changed much in Mavericks. In fact, if you've recently upgraded to iOS 7 and find yourself missing the felt casino feel of iOS 6's Game Center, you'll be relieved to find the aesthetic largely untouched.

If you've enabled iCloud, you can now use Game Center to stay in sync with your mobile gaming without plugging anything in. You can get to Game Center from your Applications folder or your Launchpad, log in, and start playing!

If you've never used Game Center before, Game Center allows users to play with and against their friends and keep track of points and achievements in game apps from the App Store. If you have an iDevice, you may notice that Game Center's icons and look and feel haven't been updated to iOS 7's graphics yet. You won't be able to play your iOS games on your Mac, unfortunately. However, a number of popular games are available in the App Store. Inside Game Center, just click on **Games** and then **Find Games in the App Store**.

Reminders

Reminders help you keep track of things you need to do. They sync with other iCloud-running devices you may use, and can be set up with tasks from Exchange, Google Calendar, and other reminder services. You can set due dates and locations to trigger reminders (meaning you'll receive a reminder either when the due date approaches or when you reach a location, if you've enabled location services). You can also check off completed tasks and keep track of everything you've already completed – remember that checking an item off doesn't actually delete it! You can create custom lists that also sync across your iCloud-enabled devices. Reminders is located on your Dock by default.

Notes

Notes uses iCloud to sync with all your devices. It's great for jotting down short messages to yourself that you can easily use across all your Apple devices. In Mavericks, you can pin important notes to your desktop by double clicking the note's title. It will pop out into its own window. Notes is located on your Dock by default.

Messages

Messages, formerly known as iMessage, lets you send a message to anyone using OS X Mountain Lion or later, iPad, iPhone, or iPod Touch. Messages uses the information stored in Contacts. To send a message, click the "New" icon and start typing a friend's name. If your friend is in your Contacts, his or her name will pop up. If not, you can send a message to a phone number or email address. You will need to be logged in with your Apple ID in order for messages to work. You can also set up Messages to enable AIM, Yahoo!, Google Talk, Jabber and Bonjour and do all your instant messaging from one place. Incoming messages will appear in your Notification Center. Messages is located on your Dock by default.

Maps

Maps is another new addition to Mavericks. Maps was introduced in iOS 6 and saw significant improvements in iOS 7. While you may not navigate with your Mac quite as often as you might with a smart phone or tablet, it's still useful for planning a route from home – especially since you can send your routes straight to your iPhone or iPad using the Share button!

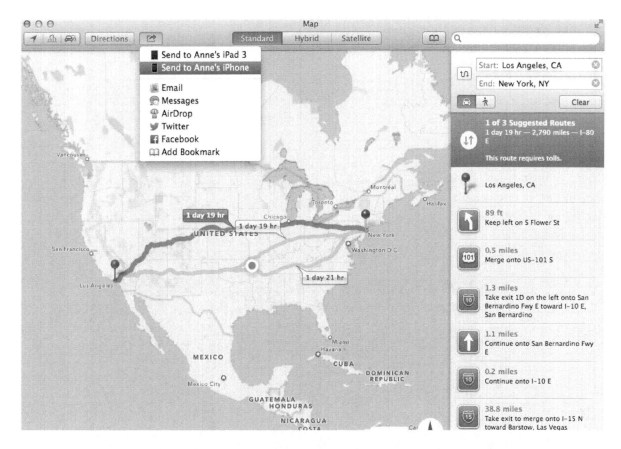

There are a number of other really useful functions in Mavericks Maps. We were pleased to discover that we could turn a map into a PDF – a portable, offline, and printable file we can move around a little more easily than online mapping services. Just click on **File > Export as PDF** to take advantage of this.

Like the iOS version of Maps, you can save bookmarked locations, see Yelp reviews for public locations, add addresses to your Contacts, and rate locations. Maps can be viewed as a standard street map, a satellite map, or a hybrid. You can also view a 3D representation of an area (FlyOver, in Apple-speak) by zooming in to near-street level and clicking the skyscraper icon in the top right. We've had somewhat mixed results with this, but it's certainly improved since the iOS 6 update in 2012.

Automator

Automator isn't new to Mavericks, but it's very useful if you find yourself performing repetitive tasks, like renaming large numbers of files. Automator doesn't require any scripting knowledge – it's a drag and drop interface for creating actions and workflows. It includes a library of actions that you can use to build your own workflows.

Automator is worth spending some time with if you find yourself performing the same set of actions over and over again. There are numerous tutorials available online, and it doesn't take very long to get the hang of it. You can find Automator in your Applications folder or by using Launchpad.

Dashboard

The Dashboard is an area of OS X Mavericks that contains several mini-applications, or widgets. You may or may not get a lot of use out of these. The default widgets are a calculator, a clock, a calendar, and a weather report. To add more or to remove widgets, click the plus or minus at the bottom left corner of the screen. You can also drag widgets around to rearrange them. You can also organize widgets into folders if you find yourself overwhelmed with too many to fit comfortably on the screen.

Dictation

To start dictation, simply press the FN key twice. You can also start dictation from any app by using the edit menu. Click **Edit > Start Dictation**. Your computer will confirm that you're about to start using dictation. A microphone icon will appear, and when you're finished, simply click **Done** or press Enter. Dictation also supports punctuation. For example, at the end of the sentence you simply say "period." It also understands several other punctuation marks. Dictation works right out of the box and uses your Mac's built-in microphone. It isn't entirely error-free, but it still does the job pretty well. As Apple enthusiastically put it, "talking is the new typing."

Mavericks also includes "enhanced dictation," though it's not enabled by default. Enhanced dictation happens in real time, meaning you can watch the words appear almost immediately after you say them. This makes a huge difference in Dictation's usefulness. To try it out, go to **System Preferences > Dictation and Speech**, and check "Use Enhanced Dictation."

Auto Save

OS X Mavericks continues OS X's proud tradition of excellent auto save, preserving the nerves of students and employees everywhere. Mavericks will automatically save your work every five minutes, and provides options for reverting to previous versions. Now you can even rename files within an app by clicking the file name in the title bar and selecting **Rename** from the menu that pops up.

NOTE: The title bar renaming feature works on most Apple apps, but may not be supported by all third party software at this time.

Screen Sharing

Improved screen sharing is one of Mavericks' best features if you find yourself doing a lot of screen sharing. Each display shows the menu bar and the dock , and you can run a different full screen app on each connected device.

Other Apps You'll Use Daily

There are a few other apps worth knowing about inside Mavericks – you'll use them all the time, but they don't have quite as much "flash" as iTunes, iBooks, Maps, Calendar, and the like. When you need them, though, you'll be glad to know they're there in Launchpad!

Preview is the app Mavericks uses to show you picture files and PDFs. It's a simple app, and most image files will open in it automatically. Nevertheless, there are a few things you may want to know. You can export image files as PDF in Preview (**File > Export as PDF**) or add annotations (**Tools > Annotations**).

TextEdit is Apple's answer to Microsoft Notepad. This is a simple plain text editor. It's certainly not fancy, but it's the kind of thing you may need one of these days.

Calculator is accessible from both your Dashboard and from Launchpad. The Launchpad version isn't quite as aesthetically pleasing, but you can have it open in the same space as your desktop, making it easier to work with numbers without having to switch back and forth from your Dashboard to your desktop.

Stickies are a love it or hate it sort of app. If you're in the love it camp, though, they're still there. Stickies are like post it notes for your desktop. Just open the Stickies app and start sticking away!

Make a note of it!

Stickies lets you keep notes (like these) on your desktop. Use a Stickies note to jot down reminders, lists, or other information. You can also use notes to store frequently used text or graphics.

• To close this note, click the close button.

• To collapse this note, double click the title bar.

Your current notes appear when you open Stickies.

3.3 Customization

It's a good idea to set up your Mac in the way that feels the most comfortable for you. This section will help you get everything set up just the way you like it.

Open up **System Preferences** (the gears icon) from the Dock. Alternatively, you can use the Apple menu in the very top left corner. This is very similar to Control Panel in Windows, and most of your customization begins here.

General Display Options (Scroll bars, Ask to Save, Recent Items)

Under **General,** you'll find some very basic options, including the option to ask to save changes before closing a document. We strongly recommend selecting this – it can save you heartache!

This is also the place where you can customize your scroll bar appearance. Mavericks hides scroll bars when they aren't in use, but if you find yourself missing them, you can bring them back under **General** in System Preferences. Select **Always** under **Show scroll bars.**

Desktop and Screen Saver

Under **Desktop and Screensaver,** you can choose your desktop background and your screensaver of choice. To choose one of your own pictures, click the **Folders** menu to expand it and then locate the image you'd like to use.

*TIP: You can also right click on any picture file in Finder or on your Desktop and choose **Set as Desktop**.*

If you'd like to use a custom screen saver, click **Screen Saver** at the top of the **Desktop and Screen Saver** System Preferences window. You can set your screen saver to one of the slideshow options and use your own photos by selecting **Choose folder** from the **Source** dropdown menu. This can be a great conversation starter at parties!

Hot Corners
If you're a former Snow Leopard user, you may have noticed that your Dashboard has moved offstage. You can access it by swiping left with three fingers, but if you'd like to reassign it to a hot corner, go to **System Preferences > Desktop and Screen Saver > Screen Saver.** Then click **Hot Corners** on the bottom right.

Hot corners trigger actions when you move your mouse pointer over to them. You can assign a hot corner to each of the four corners on your screen, though we recommend leaving the top right corner empty or set it to Notification Center – otherwise, you'll have to be very precise when accessing your notifications area. Hot corner options include Start Screen Saver, Disable Screen Saver, Mission Control, Application Windows, Desktop, Dashboard, Notification Center, Launchpad, and Put Display to Sleep.

The best way to figure out if hot corners are a good idea for you is to try them out. You can always change or remove them if they start getting in the way.

Dock Options

You can customize the appearance of your Dock by choosing **Dock** from the System Preferences window. One popular customization is to shrink the Dock's size to **small** or to hide it altogether, and then enable Magnification by checking the Magnification box. This will cause icons on the Dock to enlarge when you move the pointer over them, while saving valuable screen space when the Dock isn't in use. It's also a very aesthetically pleasing effect. Try it out!

You can also change the Dock's position on the screen, hide it altogether when you're not using it, and choose animation options for opening and closing applications. Explore a little until you find the configuration that works the best for you.

To add applications or shortcuts to your Dock, drag the application or file to the Dock and release it. To remove applications, double click on the icon in the Dock, and select **Options > Remove from Dock.** You can also instruct Mac to open an application at Login here.

Notification Center Options

You can also decide what sorts of things you want popping up in your notification center by dragging and dropping applications from "In Notification Center" and "Not in Notification Center" in **System Preferences > Notifications.** Additionally, you can turn off Notifications sounds for individual apps, control the display of notifications, and set the number of items from each app you'd like displayed by right clicking each application.

Mavericks also adds a badly needed Do Not Disturb feature. While you can activate this at any time by pressing the OPTION key and the + key at the same time, you can also set reoccurring Do Not Disturb periods (in case you want to get some sleep!). You can also specify contacts that you want to be able to FaceTime you, even if you are in Do Not Disturb Mode.

Trackpad Options

Use **System Preferences > Trackpad** to assign or change gestures according to your preferences. This is also where you can turn off natural scrolling. Deselect the "Scroll direction: natural" box under **Scroll & Zoom** to revert to "normal" scrolling.

You can also assign gestures to various tasks under **More Gestures.** Select each task you'd like to use gestures for, and then use the arrow to choose the gesture you'd like to assign.

3.4 Security and Privacy

As the world moves increasingly online, security and privacy are becoming more and more critical. Mavericks includes a number of features that will help you protect your information and your identity.

Restricting Folders from Spotlight

Let's say you use a family computer, and you've stored Christmas shopping lists on it. If you have folders you don't want Spotlight to search, click **Privacy** at the top of the **Spotlight** preferences window in **System Preferences**, and then use the + and – buttons to add or remove folders from the list of folders Spotlight won't search.

User Accounts and Parental Controls

If you will be sharing your Mac with other users, including younger children, you can create multiple user accounts and manage parental controls. The primary account (the one you used when you turned on the Mac for the first time) is also the 'Account Administrator.' The account administrator has unlimited access to all areas of the computer, the ability to install and update apps, set limits for other user accounts and more.

To manage your accounts and create additional accounts, select **System Preferences -> Users & Groups.** In addition to account administrator, you can create three other account tiers: standard, managed with parental controls, and sharing. A standard account has limitless access to all applications on the Mac. With a managed account, the account administrator has put placed limits on what the user can and cannot access. If you have a child and want to add parental limits, you will need to set up your child's account as a managed account. The files, media libraries and preferences associated with each account are stored separately from other users. You can only access your own information when logged in under your account.

To create a new account, click the (+) button at the bottom of the **Users and Groups** screen to create a new account. Enter a one-word user name. Select 'Create Account.' All new accounts default to standard access. To add administrative access, click the Security tab and select the "Allow user to administer this computer" checkbox.

If you are a parent and want to manage your child's use of the Mac, use **System Preferences >
Parental Controls.** Then customize how you'd like your child's account to access apps, the web, and
other users in Game Center. You can also set time limits, and under **Other,** hide profanity from the
dictionary, limit CD burning and printer access, and more.

Change Your Password

To set and change passwords, click the password tab in **System Preferences > Users and Groups** and
select 'Change Password.' You will need to enter both your current password and a new password to
successfully change it.

Private Browsing in Safari

Private Browsing allows you to browse the web without saving your history or any cookies or other
site data. To turn on Private Browsing in Safari, simply open Safari and select **Safari > Private
Browsing.**

App Permissions

It's easy to lose track of which app integrates with what. Fortunately, Mavericks makes it easy to
figure out which apps are tracking your location, which apps can access your contacts, etc. Just go to
System Preferences > Security and Privacy, and click on the Privacy tab. Here, you'll see a list of
apps on the left and the apps with permission to access them on the right.

3.5 Keyboard Shortcuts

OS X Mavericks contains numerous keyboard shortcuts that can make your life easier. There's no sense in trying to memorize the entire list, but it's a good idea to familiarize yourself with shortcuts that can save you time. The following table is a partial list of some of the most common shortcuts. However, if there is a shortcut associated with a task, it's generally listed on the menu next to the task's name (for an example, look at the **Edit menu** in Finder to see the shortcuts for undo, redo, copy, paste and cut – these shortcuts are useful for just about anyone!).

NOTE: This list was adapted from the extensive shortcut list found on Apple's website at http://support.apple.com/kb/HT1343

Shortcut Keys	Action
⌘+A	Select All
OPTION + ⌘ + A	Deselect All
SHIFT + ⌘ + A	Open Applications Folder
⌘+C	Copy
⌘+D	Duplicate
⌘+E	Eject
⌘+I	Get Info
⌘+N	New
SHIFT + ⌘ +T	Add to Favorites
⌘+V	Paste

⌘+W	Close Window
⌘+X	Cut
⌘+1	Icon View
⌘+2	List View
⌘+3	Column View
⌘+4	Cover Flow View
⌘+TAB	Switch Application
⌘+DELETE	Move to Trash
⌘+?	Open Help
⌘+SHIFT+Q	Log Out
⌘+CONTROL+EJECT	Restart
⌘+SHIFT+3	Take screenshot
⌘+SHIFT+4	Take partial screenshot
⌘+SHIFT+4+SPACE	Take screenshot of one window
F3	Mission Control
F4	Dashboard

3.6 Accessibility

Mavericks introduces even more features to an already-rich accessibility feature set. Switch Control allows users who cannot operate a mouse or trackpad to use a single switch device to interact with Mavericks. The built-in screen reader VoiceOver can now analyze images for vision-impaired users. VoiceOver can also duck any other sounds your system makes.

There are also a number of accessibility features that remain unchanged. You can adjust the display to enhance the contrast or to display in gray scale. You can also enable keyboard shortcuts for zooming in. Speakable Items provides a syntax for controlling your Mac with your voice instead of the keyboard.

To explore Mavericks' accessibility options, visit **System Preferences > Accessibility.**

Part 4: Maintaining Your Mac

One of the appeals of using the Mac OS X operating system is that for the most part it maintains itself. Since it is based on the Unix operating system, Mac OS X periodically runs scripts in the background that help to keep the file system in order and the memory clear. Things like defragging the hard drive are not necessary in Mac OS X. That being said, there are a few things you can do to help keep your computer running smoothly and efficiently.

4.1 Backup Your Computer Using Time Machine

There are numerous commercial and open source backup solutions available, but one of the best solutions is built into your operating system already! Time Machine will back up all of your files, applications, and settings with minimal configuration or headache. In the case of a catastrophic event such as hard drive failure, having a Time Machine backup can allow you to quickly recover all of your data and applications, and even all of your settings (such as your desktop background and even the specific location of icons on your desktop).

You will need to buy an external USB or Thunderbolt hard drive. It is recommended to buy a drive that is larger than the current used space on your computer. For example, if you have used 100 gigabytes of space on your computer's hard drive, you should buy at least a 120 gigabyte hard drive.

Simply plug the hard drive into your computer and Time Machine will start automatically. It will ask you if you would like to use the drive as a Time Machine Backup Disk. Choose "Use as Backup Disk".

If Time Machine does not start automatically, go to **Finder > Applications > Machine**, and click "Choose Backup Disk". Select your new hard drive.

After you specify the drive to use as a backup, Time Machine will automatically begin backing up your data. Time Machine will perform a backup every time you plug in the drive, or, if you leave the drive plugged in, it will perform a backup each hour for 24 hours, daily backups for the past month, and weekly backups for all previous months. When the drive becomes full, it will delete the oldest backups to make more space on the drive. That way, you can rest assured that your files are being backed up without having to interact and monitor the entire backup process.

4.2 Run Software Updates

One of the best ways to keep your computer running smoothly is to run updates as they become available. These updates fix minor bugs, make your computer more secure, and sometimes add new features to Mac OS X. It is recommended that you pay special attention to running these updates when they are available. Mac OS X, by default, will prompt you when updates are available, and you need only to click "Update" and enter your password in order to run the updates. Sometimes, in the case of major updates, you will need to restart your computer to complete the update. You can click "Not now" if you would like to delay the updates until a more convenient time.

Third-party software (for example Microsoft Office or Mozilla Firefox) will also periodically prompt you to update; it is recommended to run these updates when they become available to keep everything running smoothly and securely.

4.3 Quitting Unused Applications

To allow frequently used programs to start quickly, Mac OS X often leaves applications running even if you have closed the window you were working on. Though it makes it quicker to start these applications, if too many applications are open it can start to fill the memory and slow down the computer. To see what applications are open, simply look on the dock. Applications that are running will have a small white light underneath them. If you see an application running that you do not expect to use for a while, it is best to quit the application by right-clicking on the application's icon and choosing "Quit". You can also quit the application by clicking the title of the application in the main menu and choosing "Quit".

Alternately, you can quit the application that is currently running by using the keyboard shortcut Command + Q.

If you've had a web browser such as Safari or Firefox running for a long time and have visited many websites and notice your computer running slowly, quitting the web browser and starting it again can help free up memory and speed things up.

If an application has crashed, you can force it to quit by clicking on the Apple icon on the top left of the screen and choosing Force Quit. Then simply choose the offending application and click Force Quit.

4.4 Restarting your computer

To restart your computer, click the Apple icon in the main menu at the top of the screen and choose "Restart."

OS X Mavericks can usually run indefinitely without experiencing any problems. Because of this, it can be easy to forget to restart your computer periodically. Even if you're not experiencing any problems, it's never a bad idea to restart your computer every week or so. Restarting will allow the computer to "refresh" itself by automatically running scripts that tidy up your file system and refresh the memory. If you're experiencing a problem, a restart is often all it takes to get up and running again.

4.5 Keep your desktop and trash clean

OS X Mavericks creates a few special folders that give you a logical place to store files (for example, Documents, Pictures, Music, and Videos). You'll be best served by utilizing these folders to store your data rather than just placing everything on the desktop. In addition to the "Clean Office, Clean Mind" benefits you'll receive from having a tidy desktop, this will also put less burden on the memory in your computer and improve overall performance. If you're worried about being able to find your files if they are not kept on the desktop, remember that you can always use Spotlight to very quickly find any file on your computer by clicking on the magnifying glass in the top right of the screen.

Emptying the Trash can also help free up disk space and relieve some pressure on your system's memory. To empty the trash, simply right click on the garbage can icon in your dock and choose "Empty Trash". Alternately, you can open the Trash and click the "Empty" button at the top right of the window.

4.6 Repair Permissions

In rare circumstances, it can help to repair permissions. If you have installed many pieces of software and have run many updates on your computer, sometimes the file permissions of your operating system can become "confused," degrading overall performance.

To repair permissions on your hard drive, go to **Finder** > **Applications** > **Utilities** > **Disk Utility** (or simply type Disk Utility in Spotlight). From the Disk Utility pane, select Macintosh HD, and then click "Repair Permissions". This process may take a few minutes.

It's not often necessary to repair permissions on your computer, but it might be a good starting point for alleviating unexplained slowness or fixing problems with applications that previously ran just fine.

4.7 Getting Help

Unfortunately, sometimes app glitches and hardware disasters fail to respond, no matter what you try. When this happens, your best bet is to Google the problem. Googling a specific problem will turn up more answers, and do so far faster, than simply reading online Mac forums (though it's always nice to know you aren't alone in struggling with a problem). If you are one of the first to make the switch to Mavericks, you may also be able to find helpful work-around hints for app problems. If you don't find your problem, try posting all the details in a forum for assistance.

You can, of course, also check out Apple's online support. The help site includes a convenient search tool that allows you to explore the Knowledge Base, a collection of 100,000+ technical articles. Depending on whether you purchased an extended warranty with your Mac (known as Apple Care) you may be able to receive free phone or Genius bar support. If you call for help within the first 90 days of your Mac purchase, Apple Care technicians will assist you for free. You can also visit these sites for assistance:

Apple Discussion Groups - http://discussions.apple.com

Apple's help site - www.apple.com/support

4.8 Physical Maintenance

While Mac OS X is an operating system like no other, taking care of your physical Mac isn't too different from taking care of any other computer – but it's still worth mentioning! You shouldn't store your Mac in extremely cold or extremely hot temperatures. Use specially formulated screen cleaner to keep your screen bright and functioning for as long as possible. Keep your keyboard dust and gunk free, and watch out for spills. If you're not sure you're up to the task of keeping your Mac accident-free, consider purchasing an Apple Care warranty, which will protect against accidental damage.

Part 5: The Power of Free

OS X Mavericks comes with many applications that are great for doing almost everything you need to do. However, there are lots of free applications available that expand on your OS X's capabilities and can even mimic expensive software suites like Microsoft Office and Adobe Creative Suite.

Many of these programs are offered in Apple's App Store, making it easy to quickly get some of the best free apps available for Mac OS X.

Google Chrome

www.google.com/chrome

Google Chrome is the newest browser to enter the browser wars and has the ability to quickly synchronize information such as your bookmarks, your auto-fill information, and your browser settings wherever you use Chrome! It's been heralded for its security, speed, and ease of use compared to other available browsers. Another free browser, Firefox (www.firefox.com), is also a very popular alternative to the Safari web browser included in Mac OSX.

OpenOffice

www.openoffice.org

OpenOffice is a free and popular alternative to Microsoft's Office Suite. The full suite comes with six programs that are easy to master for anyone who's already familiar with Microsoft Office Suite. OpenOffice's applications Writer, Calc, and Impress are equivalent to the Microsoft's core applications—Word, Excel, and PowerPoint. OpenOffice also comes with programs for creating and editing vector graphics, manipulating databases, and for creating mathematical equations. OpenOffice can also save in formats that are usable by other pieces of software.

Skype

www.skype.com

Skype is a very popular app for making video calls to other Skype users, and can even be used to make calls to land lines and cell phones! Using your free Skype account, you can easily connect with video and audio to any other Skype user anywhere in the world.

Dropbox

www.dropbox.com

Dropbox is a powerful little program that lets you easily back up any file to the web, making that file immediately accessible to you anywhere in the world with an internet connection! You can also set up Dropbox to automatically back up a folder to the web (for example, your documents folder) to make sure you always have a copy of your important files whenever (and wherever!) you may need them. Dropbox starts with two gigabytes of storage for free, and for every friend you refer to the service, you receive an additional 500 megabytes of space! If you need more storage, you can buy additional storage space for a small fee. Unlike iCloud, Dropbox can handle both Windows and Mac files with no problem.

Evernote

www.evernote.com

Evernote is a great way to save anything you might be looking at on your computer. You can drag practically anything into the Evernote icon on the menu bar to have it automatically saved and cataloged at any computer you may use. Pictures, text, and even media files can be captured into Evernote for easy access later. You can even search for hand written and printed text inside of photos—great for business cards! Since it's web based, you can access these snippets anywhere with an internet connection.

Switch

www.nch.com.au/switch

Switch is the best audio converter available for OSX. It can convert pretty much any audio file format (for example, .mp3, .wav, .flac, and .wma) to any other audio format you might need. Great for getting those difficult audio file formats into an mp3! It can also be used to extract audio files from any video format (including DVDs!)

Handbrake

www.handbrake.fr

Handbrake is like Switch for video files. You can easily and quickly convert between most video formats (for example, .avi, .mpg, and .wmv) to any other format you might need. The user interface might seem a little daunting to novices, but generally if you just go with the default settings you can easily get video files into any format you may need!

ClamXav

www.clamxav.com

Mac OS X is notorious for being less virus-prone than other operating systems, however the threat of malware is always present on any system. A great, free way to stay protected from malware is by using ClamXav. You can use it to directly scan a suspicious file or to scan your entire hard drive for any malicious software - Mac, Windows, or otherwise - that might be hiding out in your computer.

CCleaner

www.ccleaner.com

CCleaner is a great little app that can help get rid of unnecessary files and can quickly clear hard drive space-hogging log and tracking files. This option rich application is the perfect tool for tidying things up, but beware: if you're not sure what it is, it's probably better not to delete it!

VLC

www.videolan.org

The VLC media player by Videolan is a standard for any operating system. It can play almost any type of audio or video file that you can throw at it, including DVDs and audio CDs, without having to install pesky plugins. In addition to providing support for those files that OS X can't support natively, its easy-to-use interface makes it the best choice for playing audio and video files.

Miro

www.getmiro.com

Miro is an open source application that acts like a media library for your computer. It mimics the style of iTunes (and can even use your iTunes information to get started), but can play many more types of audio and video files. It's also a quick way to find free streaming resources like Hulu, YouTube, and Vimeo all in one application. Unlike iTunes, which can just connect to the Apple iTunes Store, Miro can also connect to Amazon and Google Music to purchase and download new music and videos, making getting new media even easier!

Skitch

www.skitch.com

Skitch is by far the best, easiest to use, most feature-rich application for taking screenshots on OS X! Mavericks comes with a screen shot utility (press command + control + shift + 3 to copy a basic screenshot to your clipboard) that works well but might be a bit unintuitive.

You can take screenshots of your entire screen, an open window on your desktop, or of anything that you select with your mouse. By simply dragging and dropping you can save your screen shot in a variety of image formats. Even better, after taking your screenshot you can annotate the picture with text, arrows, and a whole variety of drawing tools. Additionally, you can easily upload the screenshot and annotations directly to the web, making it easy for you to share your image with others whom you give the link to!

Paparazzi

www.derailer.org/paparazzi

Paparazzi covers the one type of screenshot that Skitch doesn't take care of—taking a screenshot of an entire webpage, including the part "below the fold" where you would need to scroll down for it to appear on the screen. Though not often necessary, it helps to have Paparazzi installed for those times when you need to capture an entire webpage.

GIMP

www.gimp.org

GIMP, The GNU Image Manipulation Program, is a free alternative to the popular (and expensive!) Adobe Photoshop application. GIMP can do most of the things that can be done in Photoshop, and has a similar interface and workflow to Photoshop. It's a great choice for beginners looking to learn about digital photo editing and experienced editors who don't want to shell out the big bucks for Adobe's application.

Inkscape

www.inkscape.org

Inkscape is a free and easy-to-use vector graphics editor, comparable to Adobe Illustrator. It replicates many of the features and workflows available in these programs, without the headache of licensing fees. Great for the beginner graphic designer or anyone who needs to make a logo on the fly!

Google Earth

www.google.com/earth

Google Earth is a highly accurate virtual map and so much more! As a digital globe, it allows you to not only zoom in on specific places, but you can also take 3D tours of entire cities! In recent versions, you can even take 3D virtual tours of museums, monuments, and other landmarks. In recent versions, you can even explore the bottom of the ocean and the surface of Mars! Google Earth is a must-have app for OS X Mavericks.

Instapaper

www.instapaper.com

Instapaper will give you a read later bookmark, allowing you to save long websites or documents to read later when you have more time. For such a simple, free tool, it's wonderful for saving those things you'd like to come back to when you have more time. Instapaper is an excellent app for those who need to read a lot of documents on many different computers, but might not have the time.

CheatSheet

www.cheatsheetapp.com

CheatSheet is very handy Mac utility that displays a list of all the possible keyboard shortcuts that can be used within any app you're currently working in. Simply hold down the command key to get a quick list of all available keyboard shortcuts. Learning keyboard shortcuts is a powerful way to complete tasks in a fraction of the time, no matter what application you're using, and CheatSheet is the best application out there for learning these commands!

Unarchiver

unarchiver.c3.cx

OS X Mavericks has a built in archive utility that is great for unpacking .zip files, but Unarchiver will allow you to work with many more file formats (including .rar), and expand on the capabilities of OS X's built in archive utility. This app is a must have for any user who wants to compress (or uncompress) a set of files!

Text Wrangler

www.barebones.com/products/TextWrangler

OS X Mavericks comes with its own text editor: TextEdit. However, TextWrangler is a much more powerful free alternative that expands on the capabilities of TextEdit. Programmers and web designers swear by this application, but it's also useful for lots of other situations - for example, being able to quickly find and replace text in a file, reading obscure or old text file formats, or quickly getting rid of the "garbage" characters that might show up from reading an unrecognized format.

Quicksilver

www.qsapp.com

Quicksilver is the most complicated to use app on this list, but it's worth the effort it takes to learn how to use it. As you use your computer, Quicksilver learns your common patterns of usage and can help to quickly replicate repeated actions that you may use over and over. It also helps to streamline tasks like sending new emails and switching between songs in iTunes . Though there's a slightly steeper learning curb, there are lots of tutorials online and the payoff is enormous!

There are tons of free apps available in Apple's App Store and elsewhere online, and it never hurts to try new things out as you come across them!

Conclusion

We hope you've enjoyed getting to know your Mac and OS X Mavericks. There's so much more to explore, though, and as you become more and more familiar with your Mac, you'll discover new and exciting ways to use it that we've never even thought of. Those possibilities are just part of the fun of owning a Mac. As you develop new habits and new user needs, you'll find ways to adapt your machine to your unique personality and requirements. Mac's flexibility and ease of use will make this a fun and easy process, freeing up your mental energy for working and playing on your Mac.

You should have a good foundation for finding thousands of answers to the question, "What can Mac do for you?" - enjoy the journey!

About Minute Help Press

Minute Help Press is building a library of books for people with only minutes to spare. Follow @minutehelp on Twitter to receive the latest information about free and paid publications from Minute Help Press, or visit minutehelpguides.com.

11588236R00042

Printed in Great Britain
by Amazon.co.uk, Ltd.,
Marston Gate.